Animals in the Fall

by
Gail Saunders-Smith

Pebble Books

an imprint of Capstone Press

Pebble Books are published by Capstone Press
1710 Roe Crest Drive, North Mankato, Minnesota 56003
www.capstonepub.com

 Books published by Capstone Press are manufactured with paper
containing at least 10 percent post-consumer waste.

Library of Congress Cataloging-in-Publication Data
Saunders-Smith, Gail.
   Animals in the fall / by Gail Saunders-Smith.
      p. cm.—(Preparing for winter)
   Includes bibliographical references (p. 23) and index.
   Summary: Simple text and photographs present the behavior changes of animals
as winter approaches, such as growing thicker fur, migrating, and hibernating.
      ISBN-13: 978-1-56065-588-6 (hardcover)
      ISBN-10: 1-56065-588-7 (hardcover)
      ISBN-13: 978-1-56065-961-7 (softcover pbk.)
      ISBN-10: 1-56065-961-0 (softcover pbk.)
   1. Animal behavior—Juvenile literature. 2. Animal migration—Juvenile
literature. 3. Autumn—Juvenile literature. [1. Animals—Habits and behavior.
2. Animals—Migration. 3. Autumn.] I. Title.
QL751.5.S38 1998
591.56—dc21   97-29804

Editorial Credits
Lois Wallentine, editor; Timothy Halldin and James Franklin, designers;
   Michelle L. Norstad, photo researcher

Photo Credits
Bonefish Nature Images/Mark Morin, 10, 12
Michael H. Francis, 1, 14, 16, 18
Cathy and Gordon Illg, 4
Innerspace Visions/Doug Perrine, 8
Lior Rubin, 6
Unicorn Stock/Pam Power, cover; John Ebling, 20

Printed in the United States of America in North Mankato, Minnesota.
092012   006912R

Table of Contents

4

Geese fly south.

Some butterflies fly south.

Some whales swim south.

Deer grow winter coats.

Some dogs grow
winter coats.

Some rabbits grow winter coats.

Squirrels build nests.

Beavers build lodges.

Bears find dens.

Words to Know

bear—a large, heavy animal with thick fur

beaver—an animal with a wide, flat tail that builds dams across streams to create its lodge

butterfly—a thin insect with large, often brightly colored wings

deer—an animal with hooves

goose—a large bird with a long neck and webbed feet

rabbit—a small animial with long ears

squirrel—a small animal with a bushy tail

whale—a large sea animal that looks like a fish

Read More

Fowler, Allan. *How Do You Know It's Fall?* Rookie Read-About Science. Chicago: Children's Press, 1992.

Fowler, Allan. *Squirrels and Chipmunks.* Rookie Read-About Science. New York: Children's Press, 1997.

My First Look at Seasons. New York: Random House, 1990.

Internet Sites

FactHound offers a safe, fun way to find Internet sites related to this book.

Go to *www.facthound.com*

He'll fetch the best sites for you!

Note to Parents and Teachers

This book illustrates and describes the changes and behavior of animals as winter approaches. The clear photographs support the beginning reader in making and maintaining the meaning of the text. All noun and verb changes are clearly depicted in the photographs. Children may need assistance in using the Table of Contents, Words to Know, Read More, Internet Sites, and Index/Word List sections of the book.

Index/Word List

Word Count: 34
Early-Intervention Level: 7

24